I0081915

PHAR LAP

'Big Red' Souvenirs

JACK SPINTY

&

TOM THOMPSON

ETT IMPRINT

Exile Bay

First published by ETT Imprint, Exile Bay 2021

Phar Lap by Jack Spinty first published 1932.

A version of 'Big Red' Souvenirs was first published in *Australian Collectables* in 2005.

This edition copyright © ETT Imprint

This book is copyright. A part from any fair dealing for the purposes of private study, research criticism or review, as permitted under the Copyright Act, no par may be reproduced by any process without written permission. Inquiries should be addressed to the publishers:

ETT IMPRINT
PO Box R1906

Royal Exchange NSW 1225 Australia

ISBN 978-1-922473-47-9 (paper)
ISBN 978-1-922473-48-6 (ebook)

Cover and internal design by Tom Thompson

CONTENTS

Phar Lap with strapper Tommy Woodcock.

A Forward

Written in Sorrow

As this booklet goes to press within a few days of the death of Phar Lap, the equine miracle of the ages, one's heart mourns for the loss of a horse who was beloved of every Australian. It seems almost impossible to realise that this world-beater who was making the name of Australia ring through the world can have passed away so suddenly just when he had started to conquer the great sporting lands overseas.

Phar Lap was known to everyone. People who never went near a racecourse, men and women who hardly knew a racehorse from a heavy draught, all knew about Phar Lap and the things he had done. They had heard of him as a great racehorse over any distance and with any weight on his back; they knew him as ready and able to run on any kind of track and to win with almost any jockey on board. They knew about Phar Lap being as gentle as a pet sheep, yet endowed with plenty of spirit; they knew of him as a trier who never let up, who never showed the while feather, who stuck like a bulldog to his job and saw it through against any odds.

He was a household word too Australians; he stood in our national life as a symbol of greatness; we honored him as before his day we honored the great Carbine, because in every sense he was truly the greatest representative of his noble tribe. Phar Lap's record is an inspiration, and now his career has closed his memory will remain as a pattern and example of that pride and pluck without which there is no performance.

Jack Spinty

1

Early Days

Like many who have achieved greatness Phar Lap started life in comparative insignificance. His parents were quite commonplace. The sire, Night Raid, came from England, but his only successes in this country were made in association with novices. At this time, imported stallions of promise were worth up to 6,000 guineas but Night Raid was sold for one tenth of that sum and sent to New Zealand.

Phar Lap's dam, Entreaty, had broken down after one run. She was bought by Mr. A. F. Roberts for a mere 60 guineas. Thus Phar Lap, when foaled, was never expected to be anything out of the box. He became a gelding and seemed likely to remain unnoticed had not H. R. Telford, while on a visit to his brother Hugh Telford in the Dominion, noticed the yearling and concluded that he had qualifications which had escaped the attention of others.

When Mr. Telford returned to Australia he mentioned Phar Lap to a number of owners, but none of them were particularly interested. After all, why should they be? There were hundreds of other youngsters at least as promising and plenty who had the breeding that made them look like good investments. Nevertheless there is always someone when a bargain is on offer and D. J. Davis listened to Mr. Telford, took notice of what he had to say and cabled to a friend who was travelling in New Zealand asking him to see Hugh Telford and bid, if necessary, up to 200 guineas for the youngster.

A curious thing now happened. The friend attended the morning sale and came away under the impression that the animal in which he was interested had been sold before he arrived. There had been some confusion as to the future champion's number, and to clear up the point Davis' agent approached Telford, from whom he learned that the gelding had not been sold in the morning but was to confront the auctioneer in the afternoon. That day Phar Lap changed hands at 160 guineas; he was sent to Australia, and H. R. Telford secured a lease of him from Mr. Davis.

Phar Lap was successful in his first race carrying 8.0 in a Maiden Juvenile at Rosehill. That was in April, 1929. A little later he raced again but did no good. In the following spring he was tried at Rosehill and although the field was of quite modest pretentions he failed again. So many brilliant youngsters come along that it is hardly to be wondered at that neither the public nor turf habitues realised that the youthful chestnut was a champion in the making. Telford, keen judge that he is, however, had faith, and although many there were who laughed at him, he started his protege among the weight-for-age champions in the Warwick Stakes at Warwick Farm.

Phar Lap did not secure a place—no one expected him to— but he finished like an aeroplane with a speed and dash that staggered his critics and revealed conclusively, as his owner had believed, that he had the qualifications of a champion. Now definitely the young chestnut was on the path that leads to fame for a horse and fortune for his owners.

After the Warwick Stakes he came within an ace of downing Mollison in the Chelmsford Stakes. By this time his merits were recognised and his reputation grew like a snow ball when in succession he carried off the Rosehill Guineas, the A.J.C. Derby, the Craven Plate and the Victoria Derby.

2

When he failed in the Cup

When the Cup is spoken of in Australia it generally refers, to the Melbourne Cup, run every year in November, and it is to that event in 1929 that reference may well be made for two or three very good reasons. One is that the "Red Terror", as our overseas friends have been pleased to call him, was an early and pronounced fancy for the event; and secondly because his meteoric dash into the limelight of the Turf made him something of a type that seemed invincible. Then there was the suggestion that mistaken tactics brought about his downfall.

Those who did not see the race run held a jaundiced view, perhaps. Others who actually witnessed it tell of how he fought for his head with the strength of a lion. To have let him have his own way at the beginning of a two-mile journey would have been courting disaster. Bobby Lewis, the master jockey, whose skill and experience are beyond question, did his best to make his mount run to a plan that would get the very best from the horse when the real business began later on. Here was the experience so often to be noted among humans—the headstrong youngster w anting his own way, and the master endeavouring to get him to do the right thing for the moment.

The result was that Phar Lap was uselessly expending his energy, and when the time came for him to unwind that paralyzing run so characteristic of his finishes he could not come on, and tasted defeat just when it was expected he would triumph over all.

I was on Flemington course that day and heard the race discussed with more or less heat and assurance. Two prominent breeders were talking the race over in the shade of the members' stand. "Here is an example of the cussedness of livestock generally," said one of them.

The finish, Melbourne Cup 1929, with Nightmarch several lengths ahead of Paquito and Phar Lap in third place.

1929 Cup Day Race Programme.

"Just when you think you know all about them you discover you know nothing. If only horses could talk. If you could explain to them what is expected a t a given time in a race—how here a little patience should be observed and how they should be ready to answer the rein when the right opening presents itself, knowing that it is the rider's duty to steer out of harm's way and to move up gradually at the psychological moment, well then the really good horses would win with almost any weight!"

Then he leaned back and rocked with laughter.

"But," he added, "there would be the golden opportunity for horses and owners to put their heads together, and the last state would be worse than the first. Why I mention this is to emphasise again the fact, so frequently contended by the jockeys, that the horse beats himself as often as he is beaten by weight."

Now, looking back over the years and calling to mind what actually occurred, not a suggestion of blame can be attached to anyone. The race was one of those "turn-ups" that come in cycles, and cannot be explained by any one person to the satisfaction of everybody.

Phar Lap came on to the course that November afternoon in his usually docile manner and was walked slowly to the point from which he was to do his preliminary gallop. His condition was superb and his shining coat glinted in the sunlight as if it were satin-polished. When he turned to canter past the judges' box he appeared to sense the task in front of him and, when quietly shaken up, swept into an easy, measured stride, the perfect galloping machine. Compared with the other thorough-breds associated with him in this all-important event, Phar Lap was the gentleman among the equine plebians - well-balanced, well-groomed, and bearing himself like the genuine aristocrat of the kind.

Then they lined up, or attempted to do so. Several of the horses were a trifle fractious, nervy and shifty. Horses that are good enough to race in Melbourne Cups usually are. High-breeding, good feeding, and all the attention that pampered horse-flesh receives at the hands of indulgent stable-hands contributed to that. Here and there a spoiled darling stubbornly refused to advance to the starting gate, and several times the· red-coated clerk of the course was compelled to assist, so far as racing rules allowed, in coaxing the wayward ones into line. His difficulty was accentuated by one that insisted upon going the other way. Meanwhile the "Old Fellow" (racegoers used that term of endearment invariably because Phar Lap was so well behaved), stood still in his allotted position until the tapes flew up and a wild roar, "They're off!", from thousands of voices proclaimed from various vantage points that the struggle for supremacy had begun.

Along came the moving mass of the thousands of pounds worth of horseflesh, nostrils distended and mouths opened to the bridle bits, whilst excited spectators began thus early to pick out the positions of their fancies in the struggling mass.

Flashed here and there the colors of the riders, a strange conglomeration of splashing hues and tints, as the fighting progressed. Horses lurched forward or fell backward and ever the colors mixed in entrancing kaleidoscopic effect. In fancy one could picture a master artist splashing on a green palette pigments that were being woven into ever-changing design so the panorama spread itself to the frenzied crowd.

Thus early the horsemen were merely manoeuvring for positions. So much depended upon how the first turn would be negotiated. Fears of the spectre waiting at the corner to run an intractable animal off, or to pocket another, are ever-present with the boys who participate in a Melbourne Cup. It has been well said that "the corner" has lost for an owner more than the Cup, and won for another a coveted trophy that he did not really expect.

Taisho, another brilliant three-year-old, made Phar Lap's task much heavier as the turn was neared. Going round the turn the former ran very wide; and this left Phar Lap, who continued to fight for his head, in the van. Behind other well-known performers were bowling along nicely and were being kept in decent positions for the greater part, the unexpected spectacle of Phar Lap making his own running being a novel sight for two or three of the boys who reckoned they had more than a sporting chance. Along the back of the course the order practically was the same, and deep concern manifested itself on the brows of men who had seen this sort of thing before. The duel between jockey and horse went on until Phar Lap was allowed his head and then he opened up a gap of a couple of lengths, and there could, it seemed to the experts, be only one result. It was here that the New Zealander, Nightmarch, who ultimately won, improved his position and went up to the leader. Coming round the turn the crowd expected to see their idol wake up and begin one of those electrifying dashes that had made him famous thus early in his career. They were doomed to disappointment. The game fellow struggled on in the wake of the new leader, practically all out. Then to the surprise of every one a new challenger appeared on the scene and Paquito put in a claim, finally cutting a tired horse out of second money.

A TURF LESSON.

To the uninitiated this event proved a valuable lesson in tactics. It demonstrated that the running of races and the riding of jockeys has developed into an absolute science, and added additional value to the caution that the race is not always to the swift unless all the contestants participate under approximately equal conditions. That can never be in any horse race. Also it gives point to the remark made earlier in this chapter that a horse may even beat himself.

And what did Lewis say himself after dismounting: "Phar Lap was placed at a disadvantage by pace," he said. "It was a slowly run race and it did not suit him. He got away smartly enough but he pulled hard all the way, and ultimately I was compelled to let him go. As a matter of fact I had to let him lead from the start, and that, of course, gave the other horses in the race the better of the deal. I warned the trainer that it might be a badly run race for his horse."

WHY DISCUSS LOSING RACE?

The reason so much attention has been devoted to this Cup is not far to seek. Here was a horse that had performed well in Sydney and Melbourne before the great question was asked him. He had won both Derbies - A.J.C. and V.R.C. - and was considered early in the month to have a wonderful opportunity of crowning his already fine achievements. On the day, it may fairly be conceded, he was not on his best behaviour. It is worth mentioning, too, that on several occasions afterwards he accounted for Nightmarch, who is now proceeding to clean up in the Commonwealth what has been left to him by the champion.

3

Major Successes

His second attempt to attach the big Melbourne Cup trophy in 1930 rehabilitated him in the eyes of all those who may have formed doubts about his gameness in a searching struggle over a long distance. On this occasion he had the services of Jim Pike, whose handling of horses of this type needs no commendation. It speaks for itself. Phar Lap carried the heavy impost of 9st. 12lb., a sufficiently solid steadier for any of his tribe.

The race calls for no elaborate description. Ridden patiently and going with machine-like precision and regularity the favorite was kept in a handy position for the major part of the journey to a field that was hardly as good as that of the previous year; and when the pressure was put on him he swept along with those telling strides that were his and won with something in hand from Second Wind and Shadow King, having conceded one a stone in weight and the other over a stone and a half.

Pike, after the race, told the story he was to repeat several times afterwards. "I got away well and got him into a good position early, and then when I asked him to go on, he went." That was practically all. If not in words it was in effect.

Again one would like to know what the two breeders who had discussed the outcome of the Cup a year previously would have said if they had been called upon to deliver judgment. They would probably have reiterated the statement of a year agone, "Just when you imagine you know all about horses you discover you know nothing at all." Which, to the uninitiated appears to be queer logic, but which to the expert savors of the gospel truth. Anyhow, once again Phar Lap was placed on his pedestal by no other right than the right of merit; and that counts in the end always.

THE THIRD CUP

This brings under review the 1931 Cup, in which, weighted like a circus waggon, the champion played a rather inglorious part, finishing only eighth in a "variegated" field. The horse had been hardly himself about this time, although when he took his place in the field he showed no signs of anything being amiss. What, however, he lacked in the way of luck in not being able to place another Cup on the sideboard of his owners, he amply made up for by the number of trophies he collected in other directions.

THE DERBIES

When he won the A.J.C. Derby in 1929 he made no mistake regarding his mission, although not a few Sydney people, having tasted the bitters handed out with some persistence by the New Zealanders, had some doubts whether Honour might not be "the nigger in the woodpile". The race proved a rather soft snap for the crack three-year-old then trained in Sydney, and he led Carradale, the promising Victorian, home by 31 lengths, with Honour a mere trifle of eight lengths further away. Pike had an arm-chair ride throughout and won with almost ridiculous ease. The balm in Gilead for the Dominion people was that the winner was bred there; but the counter irritant was in the fact that he had been let go to a stranger within the gates for a comparative pittance. Be that as it may, it was small comfort to those in the land of his birth that they were unable to pick a good thing when they saw it.

History repeated itself in no uncertain measure when the V.R.C. Derby was run on the opening day of the Southern Capital's Club's meeting. The rider of Carradale once more had the discomfiture of seeing Pike's back as they finished down the straight and the consistent Phar Lap won his second "blue" within a few weeks.

A good story is told about the Melbourne victory. A young lady who had a particular fancy for Carradale which could only be attributed to the intense patriotism of the Melbournites, was being twitted by a friend - a Sydneysider - who insisted that it would be an extreme pleasure for both of them to watch the Governor's lady placing the blue-ribbon on Phar Lap's neck.

The girl's eyes blazed with real or playful indignation.

"If she does that for Phar Lap while Carradale is about, I shall wear black for a month," she retorted.

And she kept her word, albeit she went to the seaside for a month's holiday, where it did not matter much what she wore.

Taisha, who ran third in the Melbourne Derby, was the horse that behaved so erratically in the early stages of the Phar Lap Extinction Cup, as the wags of the city dubbed the race.

STAYER-SPRINTER

It is a rare occasion when one can speak of a prominent racehorse as stayer and sprinter alike, yet here was one, a proven champion, over short, middle and long distances. Who would ever expect to find a horse capable of "mixing it" in the very highest ranks of the stayers up to two miles beating the most brilliant sprinters in Australia over 7 furlongs. "The thing is unthinkable," the majority of race-goers would assert, "though of course anything is possible--anything is probable." And Phar Lap did this under the most extraordinary conditions, so far as the short distance is concerned. He carried the steadier of 10st. 3lb. in the Caulfield Futurity Stakes, and when the tapes flew up was left behind. It is estimated that he must have lost a few lengths whilst he was being got on his feet. Pike, the perfect balancer, moved him away heavily on the debit side and then, riding one of those patient, artistic races for which he is famous all over the Commonwealth, mowed his opponents down one after the other and won amidst one of the most enthusiastic demonstrations ever heard on the popular course. Behind him were Mystic Peak (no slouch over the shorter distances), and Taurus, the latter having a great "pull" in the weights. Here again was demonstrated the fact that one can't always tell from breeding or from racing itself what there is in the real thoroughbred.

Hear what Mr. James Jones, a Newcastle resident, had to say about that remarkable burst of speed: -

"I have been attending races in the different states for over 40 years. I have seen them gallop in all sizes and shapes and under varying conditions. I have seen the sprinter that ninety-nine out of every hundred would class as invincible, and until I saw this Futurity Stakes run, I was in the habit of saying that a good sprinter over his supposed pet distance will always beat the proved stayer, brilliant though the stayer may be. And now I must reconstruct theories, disentangle deductions and look at a hard cold fact that staggered me at the time. In all my years of experience I have never seen anything to approach Phar Lap's performance in the 1931 Futurity Stakes. That day he overshadowed all the sprinters, and this with a burden of l0st. 3lb., proving as conclusively as it could be proven that he was a real champion."

THE CRAVEN PLATES

On the same subject our friend went on to discuss the Craven Plate, won on two occasions - 1929 and 1930 - by Phar Lap. He considered that in winning the 1929 event the old-young-horse showed "the mettle of his pastures", as a middle-distance horse, although the time was seconds slower than was done for the "voyage" on the second occasion. The course was heavy in 1929 and the winner had opposed to him two of the finest speed machines that had up to then been introduced to Randwick. Mollison had come to Sydney with a great reputation. Indeed he had performed in both States with such distinction as to be regarded by the bulk of Victorians as unbeatable at the weights. In addition there was Amounis, another capable mud-lark and a great horse at the distance, also proven beyond all question. Phar Lap showed the way home, galloping in the mud with as much freedom as if he were on one of those fast, dry tracks that are to be frequently found at Randwick. The following· year he did better by seconds, this time disposing of Nightmarch among others.   His actual time was 2 min. 3 secs., as   against   2 min. $11^{3/4}$ secs. the year before. The 1930 time constitutes a record for Australia. Nightmarch has been looked upon as our outstanding weight-for-age performer, since Phar Lap left these shores, yet a reference to the complete list of Phar Lap's victories over him should be convincing enough as to the superiority of the idol lying dead overseas. Phar Lap made the New Zealander look a second-rater. To show the sterling quality of the Terror it may be well to mention that at   the   same   meeting   at   which   he   made   his Craven Plate record, Phar Lap came   out   and   won the Randwick Plate of $1^{3/4}$, miles, again showing conclusively, if proof were called for, that he was a champion at all distances;   and   in   the   affection   of those who love a good animal he never once   slipped from favor. Pike has well said that we are not likely to look upon his like again. High praise from one competent to speak.

THE SUNDRIES

It must not be thought that in devoting so much space to the Melbourne Cup that he did not win there is any motive behind any of the references to Phar Lap's performances.   On the contrary, it is an opportune time after the shouting and the tumult have died to review a phase of that season's racing which caused considerable and at times heated argument. The explanation made herein is generally accepted in racing circles. Further comment is needless.

It has been the endeavour   to   show   all   sides   in   the composition   of   this   famous   racehorse   by   quoting   only   the more   important   events   for   general   re view. For the most part placings   and   times   will   be   found   in   tabulated   form   in a page devoted entirely   to results. Suffice it now that we add to the list other races that have brought grist   to   the mill   and   established the fame of the most notable quadruped of all time. What other races did he win?

The Rosehill Guineas
V.R.C. Leger
V.R.C. Governor's Plate
V.R.C. - King's Plate
Warwick Farm - Norton Stakes
A.J.C. Leger
A.J.C. Cumberland Stakes
A.J.C. Randwick Plate (twice)
S.A.J.C. Elder Stakes
S.A.J.C. King's Cup
Tattersall's Chelmsford Stakes
Rosehill - Hill Stakes
A.J.C. Spring Stakes
Moonee Valley - Cox Plate
V.R.C. - Melbourne Stakes
V.R.C. Linlithgow Stakes
V.R.C. Fisher Plate
V.R.C. St. George Stakes
V.R.C. Essendon Stakes
V.R.C. King's Plate

The table will explain the details, and the total amount of his winnings will also be found in a place allotted to themselves.

He was indeed the money-spinner.

Jim Pike's racing skull cap.

4

The Horse and His Triumphs

It is difficult to reconcile the oft-repeated statement that Phar Lap was never a healthy horse with his remarkably fine temperament. It has been contended by quite a number of his admirers that below the surface he was a delicate animal, his exceptionally robust appearance notwithstanding.

On several occasions he is said to have caused his part-owner and trainer not a little anxiety, and there was a suggestion that his kidneys were not all that could be desired. To this many attribute his untimely end, since any septic trouble would be aggravated in this way.

Yet Mr. Thompson, who has been among race-horses of all kinds for years, stresses the fact that he was a "good doer" at meal times, rarely, if ever, off his feed, and as gentle as a baby. Two of his defeats when he was near the apex of his form are attributed to an illness which seems readily enough to have responded to treatment, And he always fought the issue out to the bitter end; pluck, at least, being one of his principal recommendations. He never shirked his task and not once did he curl up under pressure. This is always the hall-mark of the real champion. The harder the fight the greater the determination. And to the last Phar Lap emphasised the commonplace assertion.

One has only to remember the Futurity Stakes race, in which, after being left at the post, he carved the leaders down one by one after an exhibition of equine grit that has rarely been exemplified -

never eclipsed - on any racecourse within the Commonwealth. Nothing more on that score may be said.

LIFE ATTEMPTED

A dastardly attempt was made on the life of Phar Lap in this his own country just before the race for the Melbourne Cup of November, 1930. It caused one of the greatest sensations in the history of the turf in the Southern Hemisphere. On that occasion he was a short-priced favorite for the event, and although elaborate precautions were taken to ensure his safety the miscreants almost succeeded in their evil purpose.

On the occasion referred to when he was leaving the Caulfield racecourse after early morning exercise prior to fulfilling an engagement on the opening day of the V.R.C. Spring Meeting, several shots were fired at him, but he escaped. It seemed as if a well-arranged plan to get the favorite out of the way was frustrated by an extraordinary intervention of good fortune. Later on it must have been gall and wormwood for the conspirators to learn that the object of their wicked intentions had won the big event, starting at the shortest price of any favorite for the coveted prize.

But the attempt was a sufficient warning to Telford, who took no chances with his charge. Following the attempt on his life Phar Lap was sent secretly several miles out of Melbourne and remained in the country under guard until the morning of the race he was regarded as certain to win. Even on the course he had a strong escort of police who saw him safely to the barrier.

Another occasion upon which the great horse disappointed his admirers was when Waterline downed him in the C.M. Lloyd Stakes. All was not well with him then and it was reported that he was suffering from an internal complaint, all of which gives color to the belief that he was not the robust animal his conformation suggested. Obviously in view of the career of Waterline since that time he was not capable of giving of his best. Weight did not give him much chance in handicaps towards the close of his Australian career; and it may be taken as a commonsense view that he was close to the end of his tether so far as the big money is concerned when he departed overseas.

Tommy Woodcock with Phar Lap, San Francisco 1932.

5

Achieving Fame in America

Having won everything in sight so far as Australia was concerned, the owners of Phar Lap looked further afield. For this they have been criticised. Wiseacres have argued ponderously that Telford and Davis were not the only persons who owned Phar Lap, Australia owned him, they say. Such reasoning is trivial. Great as was Phar Lap's reputation in his own country he was a greater asset for Australia when he entered upon a career of victory in the rich Americas. If ever there was a valuable ambassador representing Australia abroad, making our name known in a way second only to the way it was made to ring through the world by the Anzacs, it was Phar Lap.

No, it was no business of any one to say, in the name of Australia, that Phar Lap should stay. It was the business of his owners and of no one else. They had won in stakes £56,440 and of course had had to pay all the usual heavy expenses to win it. For another four years probably Phar Lap would still have been a winner of good prize money, but he would have no value for stud purposes, and his owners were entitled to consider whether it was worth their while to contend for the treasures that were to be won in America and perhaps in England and Europe. Anyway it was their choice, and no man is entitled to cavil at their decision. When they sent Phar Lap overseas the best part of £150,000 in prize money was in sight for them. From the moment of Phar Lap's arrival in America - and long before - the horse was an object of renewed interest and curiosity to the sporting fraternity of the whole world. To the sorrow of all Australians and lovers of horses the Champion had trouble early with his off side fore foot owing to a stone sticking in his heel. Although in his two-mile morning exercises at San Diego he pulled up apparently sound, Veterinary Surgeon Nielsen, who was watching the horse with the utmost care, decided to operate. Phar Lap stood the operation remarkably well and a quantity of foreign matter was drained off by means of a tube. After the operation a local anaesthetic was used to help the champion in his trial training.

At this stage Dr. Freeland was favourite for the Agua Caliente handicap. This horse's prestige was increased by a sensational gallop over five furlongs which he ran next to the rails in the remarkable time of 58 seconds. Experienced men declared that they had never seen such a trial, and Australians in American racing circles were left in no doubt as to the general belief that the American horse would prove too good.

Mr. T. Woodcock, Phar Lap's trainer, however, kept the U.S.A. sporting crowd guessing by his methods of training the Australian invader. He worked his horse quite steadily, even slowly at times, in distinct opposition to the American practice, which is to gallop a horse against the clock every time he is brought out. Most Americans appeared to have the impression that the Australian was being trained secretly and merely exercised in public. One leading sporting paper, *Daily Racing Form*, came out with the following:

"Clockers believe that Phar Lap may have done some secret work on the small training track, which is half a mile distant from the main track. Many horses train there at odd hours, away from prying eyes. There is also a ring in a level dell of a canyon about 400 yards directly south of Phar Lap's stable door. Well-beaten paths lead in its direction. In this dell Trainer Woodcock obtains the green grass for Phar Lap's daily fare, and it is known that Phar Lap has visited there. A suspicion exists in clockers' minds that Phar Lap may have been a busy horse all the time he was supposed to be laid up."

The only grounds for such a theory was that Phar Lap had been taken to the dell for walking exercise and to get away from the traffic which, as trainer Woodcock remarked, was considerable when a thousand horses were stabled in close proximity.

All sorts of people visited the Australian horse in his training quarters and the interest in him grew amazingly. When Eva Novak, the movie actress who was in Australia a few years ago making a moving picture, saw this lovely link with the happy days she had spent with us, tears of pleasure and excitement ran down her face.

As the day of the big race approached, opinions about Australia's darling were very mixed. Against him were the facts that his heel had been bruised and was still not right. He did not look his best, his coat was not the beautiful satin which we knew in Australia. The small course was against him. Phar Lap had such a tremendous stride that he really needed a big roomy course like Randwick or Flemington in which to throw himself about. Racing with the off side to the rail moreover would throw the weight on his bad foot, and it was not in his favor, either, that the Americans make a habit of galloping away from the barrier at the utmost speed. On the other hand Phar Lap was a great horse - indeed the greatest of all horses full of courage and fight. The weight on his back was nothing to him and with his strength and stamina a few bumps would make no impression.

Came the day of the Australian's American debut. Fifteen thousand people were there to see the race - a big crowd for the American course. There were nine starters and the crowd cheered enthusiastically as Phar Lap with Woodcock leading him, entered the paddock. The start was held up for 12 minutes while Reveille Boy (winner of the American Derby of 1929) bucked and plunged at the barrier. At length the race started with Bahamas a popular horse, who a fortnight before had won the Agua Caliente Derby, in the lead.

As they passed the grandstand Phar Lap was seventh, his rider holding him firmly, but as the field swept round the turn into the back stretch Phar Lap, striding mightily, moved rapidly ahead. At the three-eighth post he took the lead. He increased it to four lengths by the time he rounded into the stretch. Now he was challenged by Reveille Boy who came with a mighty burst on the outside. All good American citizens started to think that the Australian would be left lamenting.

But all this time, it turned out, Elliott had been keeping a restraining hand on the old fellow. Now he let Phar Lap have his head and the Australian really began to pace it. Phar Lap's long stride is remembered by everyone, whereas Reveille Boy is "geared" much lower. The high geared racing machine soon showed that he was more than a match for the best of the opposition that day. Reveille Boy's rider worked hard with the scourge as the contenders ran side by side, but Elliott hardly did more than tickle his mount, and old Phar Lap bolted towards the post.

The Americans took it like good sports. They could have no doubt that this Australian invader was supreme, and they set up a cheer like you hear at Randwick or Flemington as Phar Lap crossed the line with two good lengths to spare.

Pulling up quickly, Phar Lap turned and cantered back while the cheering swelled to a roar. The crowd rushed to the track to admire the winner, and the police were unable to keep them back. Phar Lap was as cool as a cucumber, breathing almost normally, while all around the others were laboring from their endeavors to keep in the hunt.

After Reveille Boy came Scimitar, Joe Flores, Good and Hot, Seth's Hope, Spanish Play, Dr. Free- land, Bahamas and Cazebo, in that order.

In this his last race Phar Lap gained steady support up to within an hour of the start, the odds shortening to 6 to 5 on Phar Lap. He went to the post at evens. On the "mutuel" machines, however, on two-dollar tickets he paid five dollars for a win, six dollars 50 cents for a place and two dollars 80 for a "show". These were the best odds for a favorite that day.

After the race Phar Lap paraded in front of the judges' stand, carrying a collar of flowers hung upon his noble neck by Mrs. Leon Gordon. Cinema and press photographers took him from every angle. Elliott the jockey was nearly in tears with excitement and pleasure and, as is the custom in America, he was rushed off to the broadcasting microphone to tell the radio listeners of the world all about his ride.

Mr. D. J. Davis, part-owner of the horse, informed the press: "I was never in any doubt as to the outcome. Phar Lap showed today that he is a great horse. He will go after other rich American stakes and I am sure he will be the world's largest money winner before he returns to Australia. Woodcock did a wonderful job."

Trainer Woodcock observed that he knew he had been criticised over his methods of training, but he thought the public would now realise that Phar Lap's record-breaking performance had shown just what kind of preparation he needed. "He was better in the handicap than at any time in his life," quoth Woodcock, "better even than when he won the Melbourne Cup."

With all respect to Mr. Woodcock, who is undoubtedly a great horseman, I venture to disagree. Phar Lap in my judgment was not at top form. He would have done still better.

The U.S.A. press paid generous tribute to Phar Lap for his only American performance. The racing expert of the *New York Herald Tribune*, whose sentiments may be taken as typical, wrote in this strain:

"The sensational race of Phar Lap has no parallel in the history of American turf. It has been the lot of most foreign invaders to taste defeat, Papyrus and Epinard being examples. There have always been excuses of lack of form through climatic changes. Phar Lap not only seemed to be thoroughly acclimatised, but as fit as any horse that has gone to the post in America. His record-breaking effort at the mile and a quarter under a weight of 129lb. is all the more remarkable from the fact that there was a delay at the post. But Phar Lap is a horse without nerves, nothing worries or frets him."

As near as could be calculated, Phar Lap's connections gathered in £100,000 from the Agua Caliente win. Reckoning the American dollar as 3.65 to the £1, the $50,050 stake money was worth £13,701, and the winning bets ($US 282,700) £80,739, a total of £94,440.

That however was only a start of what appeared inevitably in sight. It was reported in the press that Tommy Gorman, the assistant manager of Agua Caliente course, guaranteed Mr. Davis £1500 in each case for the champion to make a special appearance at the

Ottawa, Toronto, Windsor, Fort Erie, Montreal and Quebec courses.

The idea was that Phar Lap be run against the time record for these courses or against horses of only moderate ability in match races. It was felt that races of this kind would get Phar Lap into that perfection of condition which would place beyond any doubt his ability to head off the American horses which he would be called upon to meet at Washington Park and Arlington Park. Incidentally it would be easy money - and after all owning a race-horse is a business and an expensive one at that.

Phar Lap, after the Agua Caliente race, Billy Elliott in the saddle.

6

The Champion's End

Then like a clap of thunder from a cloudless sky came the news by telegraph, "Phar Lap is dead", and, immediately after, poison was given as the cause. It seemed incredible, and foul play was at once suspected. It was found that an orchard next to a paddock in which Phar Lap was grazed had been sprayed shortly before with an arsenical solution for the purpose of killing insect pests. An expert of the U.S.A. Government expressed the opinion that some of the poison may have been blown on to the vegetation in Phar Lap's paddock and been eaten by the champion. Any suggestion that he had been poisoned deliberately was scouted in sporting circles and there the matter had to be left.

There could be no doubt of the depth of feeling aroused by the champion's untimely death. From all over the world messages of sympathy poured in upon the owners, trainers and all connected with the horse. The story became the chief news item of the English speaking press, it was discussed from the broadcasting stations. One American radiocaster asked listeners to stand for 30 seconds, and during that period appropriate music was played by bugle.

IN THE SHADOWS

The outstanding feature in the news of the death of this fine animal is the devotion of the men to whose care valuable animals are entrusted and the loyalty with which they perform their duties.

It would be difficult to imagine what must have been the feelings of Woodcock, the trainer, Elliott, the jockey, and Martin, the lad who rode the horse in his work, at the untimely end of their beloved friend, for Phar Lap was treated more as a member of a family than as a mere profit-making machine. To these manly fellows he was an ideal - the centre of their hopes and their affections. Cold type tells us that they cried when they looked upon their favorite stretched out in the cold grip of the harvester of horses and men. Well, it does them credit. It shows at least that no matter what the circumstance, men still have hearts that beat with the old- time regularity and that the loss of a friend in the animal kingdom is not one whit lessened because a horse has died. There are men in all communities who cannot boast the intelligence of an animal such as Phar Lap, who, though he could not speak, carried himself gracefully and decently and when tested was not found wanting. When this four-legged gentleman is contrasted with some of the brutes who masquerade as men, it is well occasionally to indulge in a little sympathy of a quadruped hero who falls by the way.

And passing on to the veterinary surgeon, it looks as if the mantle of the doctor of human beings is now spreading its folds to cover a wider field. The satisfaction to these gentlemen is that a horse makes a good patient, whatever else one may say of him, and that in ordinary circumstances he is more responsive to treatment.

THE TALES THEY TELL

When misfortune comes the way of an owner, the stable-boy may be relied upon, like the naughty boy who says the wrong things when the curate calls, to unearth his little joke. After the news of the death of Phar Lap came through and was "reticulated" to the training stables about Randwick, an open-mouthed urchin gasped, "Dinkum?"

"Sure!" replied the Peter Doody of the place. "'E's like a fellow I knew whose job it was to ride all the dead-'uns in the 'urdles. One day the boss thought 'e'd give 'im a show on a trier. Orf they goes and the mount 'its the timber and drops on th' other side. Up runs the boss and finds the jockey lookin' at 'is mount. Then 'e looks up at the boss, who had discovered th' 'orse's neck was broke.'"

"'Fair dinkum' dead this time, boss,' he says." The raconteur dodged the stable-bucket and went away to try the joke on the foreman.

It's a way they have in the Navy, also!

One last consolation is to be ours in Australia. Arrangements are being made for Phar Lap's bones, heart, head and hide to be returned to the Commonwealth for the Museum of the Australian Institute of Anatomy at Canberra. The skeleton of Carbine stands in the Melbourne Museum, the shrine of all lovers of horses who visit the Southern Capital. Soon no doubt a similar memorial will stand to a greater even than Carbine on some sacred spot where, for the next 80 or even 90 years pilgrims will foregather and say, "I remember him - the noblest of them all."

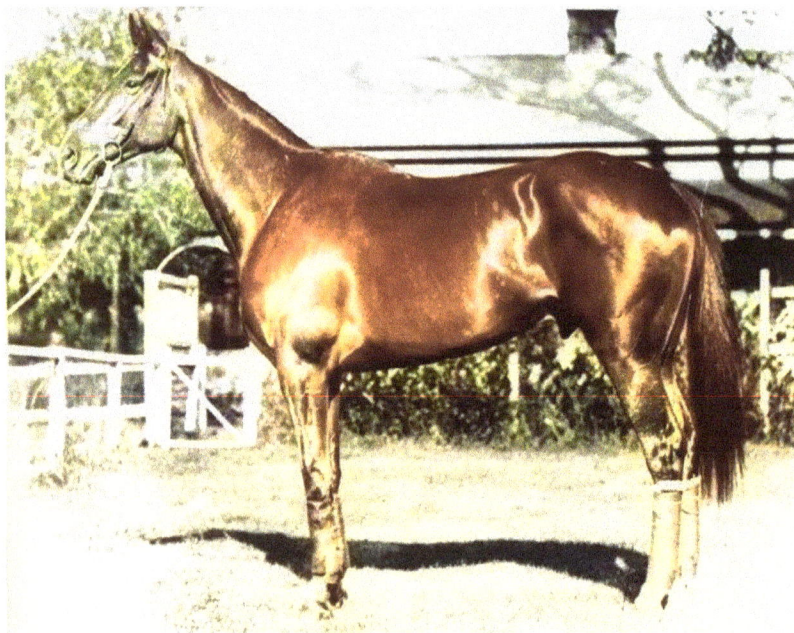

Phar Lap at Harry Telford's stables.

7

Phar Lap and Other Champions

Comparing horses of different periods never leads to much, for the simple reason that every great horse has his legion of admirers who claim theirs to be the best. But that Phar Lap was a really phenomenal horse is admitted on all sides, and I am content to acclaim him as the king of them all. Admirers of Carbine and Gloaming claim their champions had better records. When the former was racing, stakes were much below those of Phar Lap's time, as the following table will show. For instance, Carbine won the Cumberland Stakes and A.J.C. Plate three years in succession, and the total prize-money for the three victories in each race did not equal Phar Lap's cheque when he won those races once. Here are the amounts each horse received:

	Carbine	Phar Lap
A.J.C. Cumberland Stakes	£438	£1457
A.J.C. Cumberland Stakes	£445	
A.J.C. Cumberland Stakes	£425	
	£1308	
A.J.C. Plate	£472	£1451
A.J.C. Plate	£436	
A.J.C. Plate	£438	
	£1346	

But in the Melbourne Cup, when Carbine won, the race was worth £10,230, as against the £9,429 in Phar Lap's year. On the other hand, Carbine's cheque in the A.J.C. Craven Plate of 1889 came to £459;

while Phar Lap received. £2205 for his first win in 1929, and £1830 for his second a year later. So, comparing these two champions on stakes won gives Phar Lap a treble advantage in every race they competed in excepting the Melbourne Cup. The futility of comparing them on the Stakes won is therefore apparent.

Neither can they be compared as regards time for, when Carbine was racing, jockeys rode like mounted troopers-straight up in the saddle and with long stirrups.

The present-day riders now adopt what is known as the Sloan seat - that is, crouched on the withers and with short stirrups. That the present method enables a horse to go much faster than previously was forcibly illustrated to an American trainer many years ago. This trainer was in the habit of taking horses into the country centres of the States, completing what was called "the circuit". Whenever he was beaten by a country-trained horse, usually ridden by a negro jockey, he would endeavour to purchase the horse.

But what puzzled him was the fact that when he and his team returned home the horse which had been defeated would usually turn the tables on his country-trained conqueror. On his next trip round "the circuit" he again made a purchase of a negro-ridden victor over his own horse, which he regarded as a racecourse certainty. The black boy who rode the winner approached the trainer and asked to be allowed to go with the horse. Liking his appearance, the trainer agreed to take the boy too. Well, on returning home, he matched the winner and runner-up on the training track, with the usual result - his own horse won.

Then the black boy came to him and said: "You put me up, boss; I'll show you." So the next morning the nigger was put on the latest purchase and his mount won easily. Those black boys, who had never been taught to ride, often mounted a horse bare-backed, and with a piece of rope for a bridle; so they had to crouch low and hang on to the horse's mane to retain their seats. And so it was that this trainer discovered the advantage of the crouch seat as against the upright one, and instructed his jockeys to ride that way in future. The innovation became so successful that the seat of the negro boys was adopted all over America; and when Tod Sloan went to England in 1899 and rode with such phenomenal success, the advantage of the crouch became generally recognised, and is now adopted all over the world.

Thus it was left to the negro boys of America to teach the white people how to make a horse go at its fastest pace. Had Carbine been ridden by a negro, there is no telling how fast he would have travelled, but there is no disputing the fact that Phar Lap was much speedier than the champion of 1890, and how much the different styles of riding contributed to his speed must be left to conjecture.

When Carbine won the Craven Plate he lowered the mile and a quarter record to 2 min. $7^{1/4}$ sec., and when Phar Lap won the same race last spring he ran the distance in 2 min. $2^{1/2}$ sec. - $4^{3/4}$ sec. faster than the wonder-horse of 1890. This means a difference of over 80 yards, and it is open to argument whether the new seat makes that difference.

With reference to Gloaming, in one sense it might be said that he has a better race record than either of the other two; but he was reserved for weight-for-age races only and at distances no further than a mile and a half. Therefore, it would be hardly fair to Carbine and Phar Lap, who ran in handicaps and over all distances, to compare their deeds with a horse who was shrewdly kept out of handicaps, where his weight would have been considerably in excess of weight-for-age, even with penalties and allowances thrown in.

R. J. Mason, who trained Gloaming, knew every move of the racing game and with so many w.f.a. races to be won he wisely refrained from entering his charge in races when the handicapper adjusted the weights. However, a comparison of the performances of these exceptional specimens of the thoroughbred are instructive, so here they are:-

	Starts	1st	2nd	3rd	Unpl.	Value
Gloaming	67	57	9		1	£43,100
Carbine	43	33	6	3	1	£29,626
Phar Lap	51	37	3	2	9	£70,141

(Including exchange on Phar Lap's American win.)

Gloaming's only unplaced record was when the barrier broke at the start of a race and the tapes became entangled with the horse's legs and threw him. Though it is recorded as a start, Gloaming actually took no part in the race.   Carbine ran with a split hoof bound in wax-end, in the V.R.C. Canterbury Plate of 1889, and the wax-end burst during the race; the hoof spread, and Carbine dropped back last.

Records are continually being broken, and that seems to point to the fact that the thoroughbred is getting faster and faster as the years roll by, ever since the new seat has become general. Gloaming's four-furlong record of 45 seconds still holds good today, though it was made 11 years ago.   But most of the fastest times from seven furlongs upwards have been made since 1925, excepting at distances now not in use. Of the present records, Phar Lap holds two - $1^{3/4}$ mile in 2 min. $2^{1/2}$ sec., and $2^{1/4}$ miles in 4 min. $39^{3/4}$ sec.; and he was undoubtedly much superior to any of his contemporaries.

His greatest triumph was in the Melbourne Cup of 1930, when he carried the heaviest weight ever successfully borne by a four-year-old. Carbine failed at that age with 10 stone, being second to Bravo, 8.7; and yet Phar Lap won in a common canter. That he simply towered over his opponents during the last two years   is admitted on all sides, and present-day race-goers will remember him   as a veritable giant among minnows, for he made really high-class horses look like commoners when opposed to him. At the time of the last Melbourne Cup he was not in his best form, and   should   not   have been allowed to start, but his joint owners wish to keep faith with those who had already backed him, and actually started the horse against their better judgment. After his triumph at Agua Caliente, it was intended to take him to the north-eastern States to meet the best American horses, and had he lived to conquer the champions of the United States he would have gone down in history as the greatest horse of the century, not only in the eyes of all Australians, but even of Americans.

Harry Telford (left) happily lets his son hold up the Melbourne Cup on race day.

8

Phar Lap and His Riders

Nothing about Phar Lap is more remarkable than the improvement wrought in his conformation by age.

As a yearling he was just a horse and it has been said that he would not have realised half the 160 guineas paid for him on behalf of Mr. D. J. Davis at the Trentham sale but for the fact that the buyer's representative had been instructed to go as high as 200 guineas to secure him.

His appearance on arriving in Australia as a two-year-old was by no means impressive and even when he opened his winning account in a Rosehill race for horses of that age, few were greatly impressed by his looks or his galloping ability.

It was early in his three-year-old days that the Night Raid (imp.) gelding first gained fame, but it was not until the autumn of that season that students of the conformation of thoroughbreds became impressed by his remarkable physique. Phar Lap had "built up" everywhere and developed into one of the heaviest horses racing.

In spite of the increased bulk, the beautifully shaded chestnut retained the activity of a pony, and there is not the slightest doubt that the superiority he displayed over longer distances would have been as pronounced in six-furlong races had it been tested.

Unlike the usual stayer, Phar Lap carried his head fairly high, and if ever the term "bounding" was applicable to a horse's action it was to his. Even in defeat his movement did not look like that of a beaten horse, so great of heart was he.

That he gained renown by sheer ability cannot be questioned. He did his best for all classes of riders, J. Pike, J. Munro, W. Duncan, W. Elliott and J. Baker having ridden him to victory. The styles of these jockeys vary considerably, but on Phar Lap they almost invariably adopted the same tactics - just sat still, held a tight rein and allowed the horse to do the rest.

R. Lewis, doyen of Australian race riders, was on Phar Lap twice, and both times he was beaten into third place. Lack of condition was probably responsible for the chestnut's defeat in the St. George Stakes at Caulfield on February 15, 1930, while in the opinion of many he would have won the Melbourne Cup three months earlier but for the bustling to which Lewis subjected him. Such is not my own understanding of that race, as I have explained in Chapter 2.

Phar Lap, with Jim Pike up, after winning the A.J.C. Derby in 1929.

9

Phar Lap's Owners

Early in his career Phar Lap was raced on lease by H. R. Telford, but on the expiration of the contract between that trainer and Mr. D. J. Davis the pair entered into a partnership which lasted until severed by the death of the horse.

Australian racing history does not tell of another similar association of two men so different in mien, aspiration and habit. All that Telford and Davis had in common was a leaning to the turf and unbounded love and admiration for the mighty chestnut who did so much for both as well as for Australia.

An American-trained business man, Mr. Davis realises the value of publicity and is ever ready to express his views on any subject with which he is conversant. Telford can talk, too, but he is decidedly reticent, and it is only to his intimate friends that he will express his views on anything.

Davis is a clubman with social aspirations. Telford appears to live for racing and racehorses. They are married to charming women and each has a son. Telford Junr., a six-year-old, appears to be destined for a racing career, but Dave Davis' lad, who is well in his teens, is being educated for business or professional life.

Born in Victoria, Telford has had many ups and downs in life. The best horse he had before Phar Lap was Ard-na-ree, a decent handicapper, and when he approached Davis in regard to the purchasing of the son of Night Raid and Entreaty he was right up against it for cash. Today, thanks to the mighty chestnut, he is well off for worldly goods and controller of a big string of horses at his own training establishment, "Braeside", near Mentone.

D. J. Davis, on the other hand, has never been short of a few pounds - unless it was a long time ago. He made big money as an importer of high-class American cutlery to Australia and New Zealand.

In an interview just after Phar Lap won the Melbourne Cup of 1930, Mr. Davis said that the horse's earnings mattered little to him. "I have enough to live on comfortably," he continued, "but, of course, it is very nice to have the hundreds rolling in without an ounce of personal effort having to be made."

David J. Davis, owner of Phar Lap.

PHAR LAP'S STAKE WINNINGS.

AT TWO YEARS

Won Rosehill Maiden Juvenile, 6f.	£182

AT THREE YEARS

Second, Tattersall's Chelmsford Stakes, 1m. 1f.	200
Won Rosehill Guineas, 1m. 1f.	913
Won A.J.C. Derby, 1½m.	7,135
Won A.J.C. Craven Plate, 1¼m.	2,205
Won Victoria Derby, 1½m.	4,456
Third, Melbourne Cup, 2m.	1,000
Third, V.A.T.C. St. George Stakes, 1m. 1f.	75
Won V.R.C. St. Leger, 1¾m.	1,691
Won V.R.C. Governor's Plate, 1½m. ..	749
Won V.R.C. King's Plate, 2m.	1,112
Won Warwick Farm Chipping Norton Stakes, 1¼m.	747
Won A.J.C. St. Leger, 1¾m.	2,478
Won A.J.C. Cumberland Stakes, 1¾m. ..	1,457
Won A.J.C. Plate, 2¼m.	1,451
Won S.A.J.C. Elder Stakes, 1m. 1f.	325
Won King's Cup, 1½m.	800

AT FOUR YEARS

Second, W. Farm, Warwick Stakes, 1m. ..	200
Won Tatt.'s Chelmsford Stakes, 9f.	1,033
Won Rosehill Stakes, 1m.	597
Won A.J.C. Spring Stakes, 1½m.	1,462
Won A.J.C. Craven Plate, 1¼m.	1,830
Won A.J.C. Randwick Plate, 1¾m.	1,465
Won Moonee Valley W. S. Cox Plate, 9½f.	850

Won, V.R.C. Melbourne Stakes, 1¼m.   ..   1,000
Won V.R.C. Melbourne Cup, 2m.   9,429
Won V.R.C. Linlithgow Stakes, 1m.   1,000
Won V.R.C. C. B. Fisher Plate, 1½m.   1,000
Won V.A.T.C. St. George Stakes, 9f.   600
Won V.A.T.C. Futurity Stakes, 7f.   2,600
Won V.R.C. Essendon Stakes, 1¼m.   700
Won V.R.C. King's Plate, 1½m.   700
Second, V.R.C. C. M. Lloyd Stakes, 1m.   ..   200

AT FIVE YEARS

Won, Williamstown Underwood Stakes, 1m.   350
Won V.A.T.C. Memsie Stakes, 9f.   500
Won Rosehill Hill Stakes, 1m.   444
Won A.J.C. Spring Stakes, 1½m.   779
Won A.J.C. Craven Plate, 1¼m.   940
Won A.J.C. Randwick Plate, 2m.   740
Won Moonee Valley W. S. Cox Plate, 9½f.   500
Won V.R.C. Melbourne Stakes, 1¼m.   525
Won Agua Caliente Handicap, 1¼m. *13,701

£70,141

* Exchange included.

1 1

Phar Lap - His Pedigree

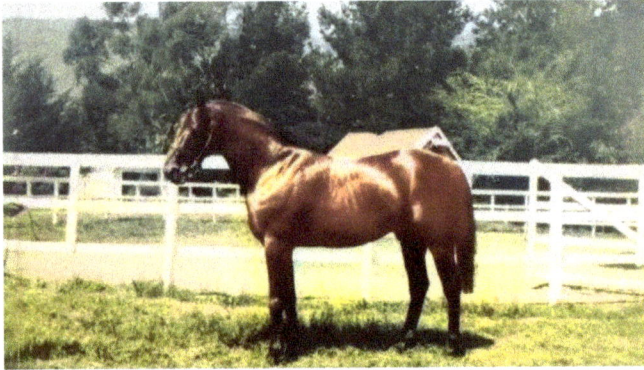

your Lucky Breed Try it again

DAM OF PHAR LAP SOLD FOR 1000 GUINEAS

Bobbie No 2

(Top): Nightraid, and below: Entreaty with foal, a full-brother to Phar Lap.

The Champion's Pedigree

PHAR LAP

	Night Raid			Entreaty

ENTREATY (2)	WINKIE (Imp.) 1	William the Third 2	St. Simon	Galopin 3
				St. Angela 11
			Gravity	Wisdom 7
				Enigma 2
		Conjure	Juggler 9	Touchet 14
				Enchantress 9
			Connie	Pero Gomez 27
				Hilarity 1
	PRAYER WHEEL	Pilgrim's Progress 1	Isonomy 19	Sterling 12
				Isola Bella 19
			Pilgrimage •	The Earl or The Palmer 5
				Lady Analey 1
		Catherine Wheel	Maxim 12	Musket 3
				Realisation 12
			Misskate (imp.)	Adventurer 12
				Sporting Life 2

NIGHT RAID, B. H., 1918 (1)

RADIUM 3	Bend Or 1	Doncaster 5	Stockwell 3	The Baron 24	Birdcatcher 11 / Echidna by Economist 36
				Pocahontas	Glencoe 1 / Marpessa, by Muley 6
			Marigold	Teddington 2	Orlando 13 / Miss Twickenham, by Rockingham 24
				S. to Singapore	Ratan 9 / Daughter of Melbourne 1
		Rouge Rose	Thormanby 4*	Windhound 3	Pantaloon 17 / Phryne, by Touchstone 14
				Alice Hawthorn	Muley Moloch 9 / Rebecca, by Lottery 11
			Ellen Horne	Redshank 1	Sandbeck 8 / Johanna, by Selim 2
				Delhi	Plenipotentiary 6 / Pawn Junior, by Waxy 18
	Taia	Donovan 7	Galopin 3	Vedette 19	Voltigeur 2 / Mrs. Ridgway, by Birdcatcher 11
				The Flying Duchess	The Flying Dutchman 3 / Merope, by Voltaire 12
			Mowerina	Scottish Chief 12	Lord of the Isles 4 / Miss Ann, by The Little Known 1
				Stockings	Stockwell 3 / Go Ahead, by Melbourne 1
		Eira	Kisber 4	Buccaneer 14	Wild Dayrell 7 / Dau. of Little Red Rover 37
				Mineral	Rataplan 3 / Manganese, by Birdcatcher 11
			Æolia	Parmesan 7	Sweetmeat 21 / Gruyere, by Verulam 1
				Breeze	King Tom 3 / Mentmore Lass, by Melbourne 1
SENTIMENT	Spearmint 1	Carbine 2	Musket 3	Toxophilite 3	Longbow 21 / Legerdemain, by Pantaloon 17
				Daughter of	West Australian 7 / Brown Bess, by Camel 24
			Mersey	Knowsley 3	Stockwell 3 / Daughter of Orlando 13
				Clemence	Newminster 8 / Eulogy, by Euclid 7
		Maid of the Mist	Minting 1	Lord Lyon 1	Stockwell 3 / Paradigm, Paragone 2
				Mint Sauce	Young Melbourne 25 / Sycee, by Marsyas 12
			Warble	Skylark 15	King Tom 3 / Wheatear, by Young Melbourne 25
				Coturnix	Thunderbolt 11 / Fravolina, by Orlando 13
	Flair	St. Frusquin 22	St. Simon 11	Galopin 3	Vedette 19 / The Flying Duchess, by The Flying [Dutchman 3
				St. Angela	King Tom 3 / Adeline, by Ion 4
			Isabel	Plebeian 11	Joskin 5 / Queen Elizabeth, by Autocrat 1
				Parma	Parmesan 7 / Archeress, by Longbow 21
		Glare	Ayrshire 8	Hampton 10	Lord Clifden 2 / Lady Langden, by Kettledrum 3
				Atalanta	Galopin 3 / Feroma, by Thormanby 4*
			Footlight	Cremorne 2	Parmesan 7 / Rigolboche, by Rataplan 3
				Paraffin	Blair Athol 10 / Paradigm, by Paragone 2

PHAR LAP'S RECORD.

AT TWO YEARS.

Unp., 6.11, Feb. 23, Rosehill Nursery, 5½f. Exact, 8.6, 1. Time, 1.7¾.

Unp., 7.3, March 2, Hawkesbury Two-Year-Old, 5f. Sheila, 7.10, 1. Time, 1.4.

Unp., 6.7, March 16, Rosehill Nursery, 6f. My Talisman, 6.13, 1. Time 1.15¼.

Unp., 7.6, April 1, A.J.C. Easter Stakes, 7f. Carradale, 8.2, 1. Time, 1.26½.

First, 7.9 (J. Baker), April 27, Rosehill Maiden Juvenile, 6f. Voleuse, 7.6, 2; Pure Tea, 8.12, 3. Half length. Time, 1.15½.

AT THREE YEARS.

Unp., 7.2, Aug. 3, W. Farm Denham Court Hcp., 6f. Killarney, 8.13, 1. Time, 1.13.

Unp., 7.13, Aug. 17, Rosehill Three-Year-Old, 7f. Firbolg, 8.10, and King Crow, 8.7 (dead heat), 1. Time, 1.27¾.

Unp., 7.6, Aug. 24, Rosehill Three and Four-Yr.-Old, 7f. Ticino, 8.3, 1. Time, 1.27.

Unp., 7.6, Aug. 31, Warwick Farm Stakes, 1m. Limerick, 9.0, 1. Time, 1.38¾.

Second, 7.6, Sept 14, Tattersall's Chelmsford Stakes, 9f. Mollison, 9.4, 1; Winalot, 9.11, 3. Half length. Time, 1.52.

First, 8.5 (J. Munro), Sept. 21, Rosehill Guineas, 9f. Lorason, 8.5, 2; Holdfast, 8.5, 3. Three lengths. Time, 1.52.

First, 8.10 (J. Pike), Oct. 5, A.J.C. Derby, 1½m. Carradale, 8.10, 2; Honour, 8.10, 3. Three and a half lengths. Time, 2.31¼.

First, 7.8 (W. Duncan), Oct. 9, A.J.C. Craven Plate, 1¼m. Mollison, 8.11, 2; Amounis, 9.1, 3. Four lengths. Time, 2-11¼.

First, 8.10 (J. Pike), Nov. 2, V.R.C. Derby, 1½m. Carradale, 8.10, 2; Taisho, 8.10, 3. Two lengths. Time, 2.31¼.

Third, 7.6 (R. Lewis), Nov. 5, Melbourne Cup, 2m. Nightmarch, 9.2, 1; Paquito, 8.5, 2. Three lengths, length. Time, 3.26½.

Third, 8.10 (R. Lewis), Feb. 15, V.A.T.C. St. George Plate, 9f. Amounis, 9.9, 1; Parsee, 9.2, 2. Half length, neck. Time, 1.53¾.

First, 8.10 (J. Pike), March 1, V.R.C. St. Leger, 1¾m. Sir Ribble, 8.10, 2; Lineage, 8.7, 3. Three-quarters of a length. Time, 3.1¼.

First, 7.13 (W. Elliott), March 6, V.R.C. Governor's Plate, 1½m. Lineage, 7.13, 2; High Syce, 9.3, 3. Four lengths. Time, 2.30¼.

First, 7.11 (W. Elliott), March 8, V.R.C. King s Plate. Second Wind, 8.11, 2; Lineage, 7.11, 3. Twenty lengths. Time, 3.25.

First, 8.10 (J. Pike), April 12, W. Farm Chipping Norton Stakes, 1¼m. Amounis, 9.6, 2; Nightmarch, 9.7, 3. Two lengths. Time, 2.6.

First, 8.10 (J. Pike), April 19, A.J.C. St. Leger, 1¼m. Sir Ribble, 8.10, 2; Peacemaker, 8.10, 3. Three and a half lengths. Time, 3.7.

First, 8.1 (W. Elliott), April 23, A.J.C. Cumberland Stakes, 1¾m. Donald, 9.0, 2; Kidaides, 9.0, 3. Two lengths. Time, 2.58¾.

First, 7.13 (W. Elliott), April 26, A.J.C. Plate, 2¼m. Nightmarch, 9.0, 1; Donald, 9.1, 3. Ten lengths. Time, 3.49½.

First, 8.4 (W. Elliott), May 10, S.A.J.C. Elder Stakes, 9f. Fruition, 8.13, 2. Five lengths. Time, 1.52.

First, 9.5 (J. Pike), May 17, S.A.J.C. King's Cup, 1½m. Nadean, 8.2, and Kirrkie, 7.10, dead-heat, 2. Three and a half lengths. Time, 2.34.

AT FOUR YEARS.

Second, 8.11 (J. Pike), Aug. 30, Warwick Farm Stakes, 1m. Amounis, 9.0, 1; Nightmarch, 9.3, 3. Short head. Time, 1.38.

First, 9.4 (J. Pike), Sept. 13, Tattersall's Chelmsford Stakes, 9f. Nightmarch, 9.11, 2; Weotara, 7.6, 3. Two and a half lengths. Time, 1.51½.

First, 9.4 (J. Pike), Sept. 20, Rosehill Hill Stakes, 1m. Nightmarch, 9.3, 2; High Disdain, 9.0, 3. Length. Time, 1.40.

First, 8.11 (J. Pike), Oct. 4, A.J.C. Spring Stakes, 1½m. Nightmarch, 9.5, 2; Concentrate, 9.2, 3. Half length. Time, 2.33¼.

First, 8.11 (J. Pike), Oct. 8, A.J.C. Craven Plate, 1¼m. Nightmarch, 9.4, 2; Donald, 9.2, 3. Six lengths. Time, 2.3.

First, 8.11 (J. Pike), Oct. 11, A.J.C. Randwick Plate, 2m. Donald, 9.4, 2; Concentrate, 9.3, 3. Two lengths. Time, 3.36$\frac{1}{4}$.

First, 8.11 (J. Pike), Oct. 25, M. Valley W. S. Cox Plate, 9$\frac{1}{2}$f. Tregilla, 7.11, 2; Mollison, 9.1, 3. Four lengths. Time, 1.59$\frac{1}{4}$.

First, 8.11 (J. Pike), Nov. 1, V.R.C. Melbourne Stakes, 1$\frac{1}{4}$m. Tregilla, 7.12, 2; Amounis, 9.0, 3. Three lengths. Time, 2.4$\frac{1}{2}$.

First, 9.12 (J. Pike), Nov. 4, Melbourne Cup, 2m. Second Wind, 8.12, 2; Shadow King, 8.4, 3. Three lengths. Time, 3.27$\frac{3}{4}$.

First, 8.12 (J. Pike), Nov. 6, V.R.C. Linlithgow Stakes, 1m. Mollison, 8.13, 2; Mystic Peak, 9.2, 3. Four lengths. Time, 1.37.

First, 8.12 (J. Pike), Nov. 8, V.R.C. C. B. Fisher Plate, 1$\frac{1}{2}$m. Second Wind, 9.1, 2; Lineage, 9.1, 3. Three and a half lengths. Time, 2.48$\frac{1}{4}$.

First, 9.7 (J. Pike), Feb. 14, V.A.T.C. St. George Stakes, 9f. Induna, 8.3, 2; Glare, 8.13, 3. Two and a half lengths. Time, 1.54$\frac{3}{4}$.

First, 10.3 (J. Pike), Feb. 21, V.A.T.C. Futurity Stakes, 7f. Mystic Peak, 10.2, 2; Taurus, 8.12, 3. One and a half lengths. Time, 1.27$\frac{1}{4}$.

First, 9.7 (J. Pike), Feb. 28, V.R.C. Essendon Stakes, 1$\frac{1}{4}$m. Lampra, 8.0, 2; Mira Donna, 7.7, 3. Three lengths. Time, 2.5$\frac{1}{2}$.

First, 9.7 (J. Pike), March 4, V.R.C. King's Plate, 1$\frac{1}{2}$m. Glare, 8.3, 2; El Rey, 8.3, 3. One and a quarter lengths. Time, 2.37$\frac{1}{4}$.

Second, 9.7 (J. Pike), March 7, V.R.C. C. M. Lloyd Stakes, 1m. Waterline, 8.0, 1; Temoin, 8.0, 3. Neck. Time, 1.38.

AT FIVE YEARS.

First, 9.0 (W. Elliott), Aug. 25, Williamstown Underwood Stakes, 1m. Rondalina, 7.6, 2; Wise Force, 9.3, 3. One and three-quarter lengths. Time, 1.42½.

First, 9.8 (J. Pike), Sept. 5, V.A.T.C. Memsie Stakes, 9f. Rondalina, 6.11, 2; Waterline, 9.8, 3. Three and a half lengths. Time, 1.52¾.

First, 9.0 (J. Pike), Sept. 19, Rosehill Hill Stakes, 1m. Chide, 9.0, 2; Waugoola, 9.0, 3. One and a half lengths. Time, 1.39½.

First, 9.2 (J. Pike), Oct. 3, A.J.C. Spring Stakes, 1½m. Chide, 9.3, 2; The Dimmer, 9.3, 3. One and a quarter lengths. Time, 2.33¾.

First, 9.1 (J. Pike), Oct. 7, A.J.C. Craven Plate, 1¼m. Pentheus, 9.4, 2; Chide, 9.1, 3. Four lengths. Time, 2.2½.

First, 9.3 (J. Pike), Oct. 10, A.J.C. Randwick Plate, 2m. Chide, 9.4, 2. Four lengths. Time, 3.31.

First, 9.4 (J. Pike), Oct. 24, M. Valley W. S. Cox Plate, 9½f. Chatham, 7.11, 2; Johnnie Jason, 7.11, 3. Two and a half lengths. Time, 2.1¼.

First, 9.1 (J. Pike), Oct. 31, V.R.C. Melbourne Stakes, 1¼m. Concentrate, 9.1, 2; Veilmond, 9.0, 3. Half length. Time, 2.6½.

Unp., 10.10 (J. Pike), Nov. 3, Melbourne Cup, 2m. White Nose, 6.12, 1; Shadow King, 8.7, 2; Concentrate, 8.10, 3. Time, 3.26.

First, 9.3 (W. Elliott), March 20, Agua Caliente (Mexico) Handicap, 1¼m. Reveille Boy, 8.6, 2; Scimitar, 7.2, 3. Two lengths. Time, 2.2-4/5.

RECORD (51 starts)—37 firsts, 3 seconds, 2 thirds, 9 times unplaced.

1 3

'Big Red' Souvenirs

Phar Lap is one of the handful of Australian sporting icons whose singular record of achievement - like Bradman's – will never diminish. He hit a cultural nerve with the public so much so that his legend lives on making Phar Lap memorabilia very collectable. As with Bradman, the souveniring began over 70 years ago.

On 20 March 1932, Phar Lap won the world's richest horse race, the US$50,000 Agua Caliente Handicap in Mexico, a race that occurred within 24 hours of the opening of the Sydney Harbour Bridge. America hailed the records of Big Red, the galloping kangaroo.

Both achievements had been Australian success stories during the bitter times of economic depression and followed Don Bradman's world record score of 452 not out. Bradman has gone, that record has gone, but the Bridge still stands – and Phar Lap too.

After his death, just 16 days after beating America's greatest horses, his owners decided to celebrate Big Red in a stunning trifecta of memorials. His huge 14lb heart was preserved, bottled and lodged in the National Museum of Anatomy in Canberra (it is now in the National Museum of Australia). His hide was treated by a taxidermist and sent to the Museum of Victoria. His skeleton was sent to the Dominion Museum in Wellington (now the Museum of New Zealand) – all to satisfy the public interest.

Phar Lap has become ultimately collectable, positively totemic and not just in Australia and New Zealand. In July 2003, racing collectors in the USA were offered the lucky kangaroo-skin saddle used by jockey Bill Elliot when he rode Phar Lap in the Caliente Handicap.

Elliot gave the saddle to fellow jockey George Woolf in 1932. Woolf used this saddle in all his rides on the great American race horse Seabiscuit, who, like Phar Lap, was the subject of a feature film. The saddle sold for US$125,000 in 2003 and is now on loan to the National Racing Museum and Hall of Fame in Saratoga Springs.

In 2004, another Elliot saddle was bought for $87,000 in Melbourne in a joint effort by the Federal Government ($25,000), the Victorian Government ($50,000) and the Australian Racing Museum ($12,000). Described as the saddle used by Bill Elliot to win 'seven races from seven starts, including his final race at Agua Caliente', it seems that Phar Lap must have been doubly mounted in Mexico!

Billy Elliot's Phar Lap saddle at Museums Victoria.

The reverence for Phar Lap memorabilia can be easily established as so little enters the market. Yet following a tip in October 2004, I uncovered 14 personal items in far north Queensland. A silk blouse race worn by both Jim Pike and Elliot; Elliot's own inscribed race book for Agua Caliente; sections of the floral presentation and photographs on card of the final event.

This silk blouse, shared by Pike and Elliot, sold for $67,700 in 2005.

During 1929 and 1930, Pike and Elliot both wore the silks we received from the first Mrs Elliot. The deep red racing blouse has black and white armbands, with some fraying to the silk sections of both lower sleeves, and evidence of mud. Pike wore this silk when he first rode Phar Lap in the AJC Derby (5.10.1929), then in the Victoria Derby (2.11.1929), and again for first place in the VRC St Leger Stakes (1.3.1930). He handed it on to Bill Elliot when Phar Lap won the Governor's Plate (6.3.1930), the King's Plate (8.3.1930), the Cumberland Stakes (23.4.1930), the AJC Plate (26.4.1930) and the Elder Stakes (10.5.1930).

Billy Elliot's Lucky saddle as used by George Woolf with Seabiscuit, now in Saratoga Springs.

Pike's next ride on Phar Lap was the King's Cup on 17 May 1930, where a new slim-line blouse with three black bands was on show (see the *Referee*, 21 March 1930). Telford probably passed these silks around to his other jockeys in 1929 This would add another two first place rides for Big Red, but my feeling is that Telford held on to the silks used by Lewis when he rode Phar Lap into third place in the 1929 Melbourne Cup.

Anecdotal evidence and family lore has it that Elliot took these silks in his luggage to America, intending to use them. But on finding another horse with similar colours, Telford changed Phar Lap's colours for that one last ride.

McCarten had an original sepia photograph of Night March winning the 1929 Melbourne Cup, ahead of Paquito (McCarten) and Phar Lap (Lewis). McCarten himself inscribed these details on the reverse. Perhaps it is worth only a few hundred dollars, but out-gunning the wonder horse meant a lot to the jockey.

Pike finally got Big Red over the line in the 1930 Melbourne Cup. Souvenir tinplates of the pair were created by Agnew & Company that Christmas. Pike won 22 races in a row on Big Red, before coming eighth in the 1931 Cup under the horrible weight of 68 kg. This prompted Telford to take the horse to America when he wrapped up his Randwick stables.

Jim Pike then passed on Phar Lap's small zinc alloy stable nameplate from Randwick to his favourite barber, Carl Phillips in nearby Zetland. He put it on a lean-to in Leichhardt for over 20 years before putting it in a cupboard out of the driving rain.

Another special item is an original Agua Caliente race book for 20 March 1932. Bill Elliot's copy of the Official Program of the Agua Caliente Jockey Club should not be confused with the pre-race souvenir booklet that is in the Museum of Victoria, which shows the race being billed as $100,000. When the Depression hit the racing industry, the prize money was halved.

Elliot had folded over his 18-page program to Race Thirteen – the Agua Caliente Handicap, noting the first four place-getters and Phar Lap's record race time. He pasted the program down onto a section of the hard floral presentation card he received after the race. While Race Thirteen is rather faded, the race program front page has been protected with its clear inscription: 'To my Darling Wife, with best love from Bill.' Surely this is the ultimate association copy (see below).

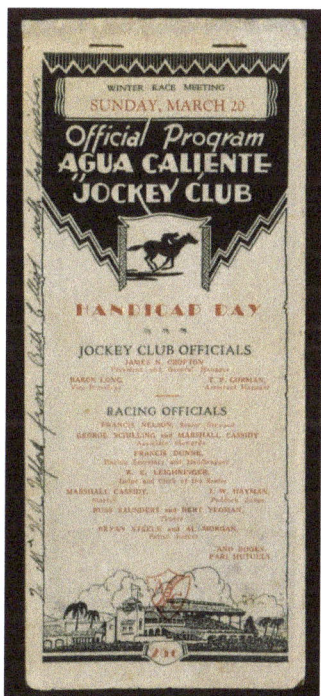

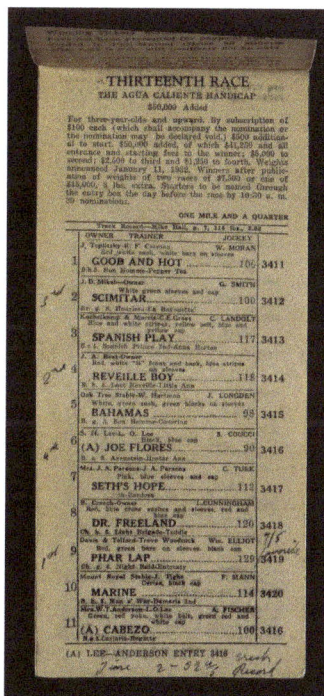

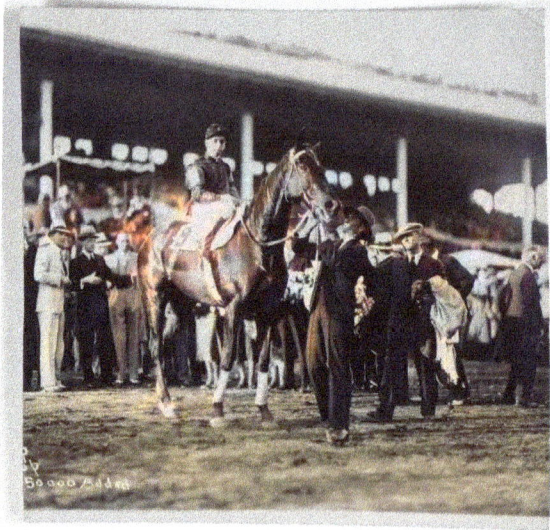

A fine but cropped copy of Elliot on Phar Lap after the Agua Caliente success.

With the silks came a lovely bundle of original sepia photographs, each about 16.4 x 12 cm, each pasted down on card, numbered and dated '3.20.32 A.C. Handicap – 50,000 Added'. Each shows scenes from Phar Lap's last race. Big Red beat America's favourite Reveille Boy who had just won the Kentucky Derby.

Four of these photographs covered developments in the race, while another group shows Elliot on Phar Lap, with strapper Tommy Woodcock, directly after the race. In one, a jubilant, lanky Woodcock is leading Phar Lap over to the floral presentation. Another shows jockey Elliot surrounded by well-wishers, including owner David Davis and Hollywood actress Billie Burke. Davis had film connections in California and had arranged with Laski & Co to film the race to promote the horse in future races across America.

The original hand-written presentation card, about 16 cm across, is rather poignant: 'AGUA-CALIENTE HCP & FLORAL PRESENTATION – W. Elliot up – March 20th. 1932'. Hastily done, Phar Lap fails to be named despite being hailed as the world's greatest galloper by such public figures as writer Damon Runyon:

'Suddenly he began covering ground in great leaps like a mammoth kangaroo and he soon overhauled the field and won by much open daylight.'

And that was his last outing on his first dirt track!

Newspapers took a great interest in the race. A special issue of *The Australasian* for 26 March 1932 included colour pages on the Sydney Harbour Bridge opening, a full page on Phar Lap in colour, and the article, 'Phar Lap The Wonder Horse' on his Agua Caliente race win.

Within days of Phar Lap's death, New Century Press published Jack Spinty's book *Phar Lap: the record breaker*, from their office under the southern pylon of the new Sydney Harbour Bridge. This 64-page booklet included nine full-page photographs, a poem by Colin Wills, together with Phar Lap's full pedigree and race results to Agua Caliente. This first book on Phar Lap has proved to be extremely scarce. The National Library of Australia finally received a copy in December 2004 by donation. The State Library of NSW has had to make do with a 1987 reprint.

THE RECORD BREAKER
PHAR LAP
GREATEST
OF ALL RACE HORSES
PRICE ONE SHILLING

At the winning post, 1930 Melbourne Cup.
Tommy Woodcock gives Phar Lap a training run 1932.

An amber glass trophy of Phar Lap's head is equally rare. It stands about 13 cm high on an oval base, with raised letters PHAR LAP and 1928-1932 on one side, '37 wins from 51 starts' on the other. One of only eight known to have been made in 1932, this one below is in perfect condition and was owned by Sydney bookmaker Joe Taylor. While others have been sighted, they usually have chipped ears, and retain fragments of their green felt base. Originally fitted within a small cedar box, this edition was made by Tooth's Brewery management as a personal memento to a select few in the racing fraternity. I have only sighted one example of the clear glass variety (below).

The presence of Phar Lap's remains in the national museums of both Australia and New Zealand confirms how important he is as a cultural icon in both countries. The newly discovered Phar Lap memorabilia was sold by Lawson Menzies in Sydney on 4 April 2005, and were taken on by major institutions. Further to these finds, both Lawsons and Leskis also offered up Phar Lap racing shoes with strong provenance, even a nail from one of these shoes (originally offered up by Tommy Woodcock at an Emerald auction forty years ago) found a new home.

Phar Lap racing shoes, the one above rebuilt in preparation for Agua Caliente.

The earliest known Phar Lap shoe, acquired by Grange Waterson, the under-bidder to Telford at Trentham. A nail from a Phar Lap shoe first offered in Emerald in 1977 by Tommy Woodcock; and a good example of provenance attached to the sale of Phar Lap racing plate.

Jockey Jim Pike died penniless in a Bondi flat, one entirely papered with Phar Lap newspaper cutting, photographs, betting slips, and fan letters. Regrettably these were removed and taken to the local tip. Following his death, all of his own gear - saddles, bridles, whips et al - were sent to his estranged wife Olga Pike, who sold everything to Roger East, a stud owner in Victoria. The entire grouping went on to jockey Reg Howarth of Tahoma Stud and most of these items were offered at Cromwell's auction house in 2005. The National Museum of Australia purchased several items including Pike's whip, boots and skull cap, some of which can be seen below.

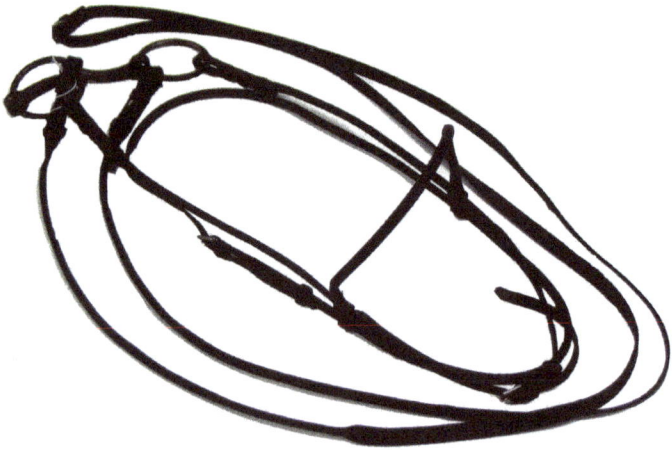

Phar Lap's Melbourne Cup 1930 saddle.
A Phar Lap bridle, both originally owned by Jim Pike.

Finally we should also look out for Phar Lap race day programmes, as these have very much increased in value and rarity in the last ten years. The highest prices are reserved to the 1930 Melbourne Cup and Agua Caliente programmes, these being about $12,000 and $20,000 respectively. Prices are less without covers, fading or sunned covers, or extensive notes within, when not in pencil.

The New Zealand Thoroughbred Yearling Sale book 1927 (see below)is highly in demand as it holds the first description of the great horse when purchased by Harry Telford for 160 guineas.

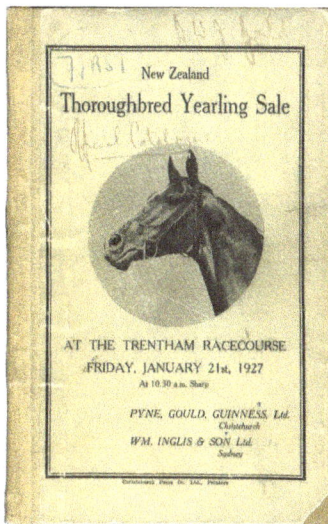

15600

DERBY DAY.

VICTORIA RACING CLUB

Spring Meeting
1929.

Official Programme.

Arthur H. Kearney Sec.

PRICE ONE SHILLING.

REGISTERED UNDER THE COPYRIGHT ACT.

VICTORIA DERBY
(CONTINUED)

		at lb
6	PHAR-LAP Mr. H. R. Telford's ch g ..	8 10
	Night Raid—Entreaty [Owner]	
	Red, black and white hooped sleeves, red cap	
	Barrier 5 Rider R. Lewis	
7	THIRD KING Mr. H. H. Kerr's br c ..	8 10
	King Ingoda—Mnemonic [S. Cawdia]	
	Black, white cross sashes, sleeves and cap	
	Barrier 7 Rider Woodlet	

UNLIKELY STARTER

8	— Mr. J. W. Cormack's b c	8 10
	Lord Quex—Retraction	
	Barrier 1 Rider................	

Time 2 Min 31½ Sec.

MOONEE VALLEY
RACING CLUB

Official Programme
PUBLISHED BY AUTHORITY.

PRICE, ONE SHILLING

CUP MEETING.
SATURDAY, 24th OCTOBER, 1931.

A. V. HISKENS, SEC.

Sold on the Course, 1/- Each

This Book is compiled and carefully checked by the Club's officers, if by any insertions the inaccurate the child will Numbers it.

F. S. Trueboot, Printer, 85 Hardware St., Melbourne.

THE W. S. COX PLATE.
3.15 p.m.

Of £750 (including Trophy value £100). Second horse to receive £150 and the third horse £100 from the stake. For 3-years-old and upwards. Standard weight for age. (No allowance to geldings.) Nomination, £1. Acceptance, £6.

Nine and a Half Furlongs.

			yrs. st. lb.
1	PHAR LAP Messrs. D. J. Davis & H. R. Telford's ch g	5 9 4	
	Night Raid—Entreaty [H. R. Telford]		
	Red, red and green hooped sleeves, black cap.		
	Barrier Position 8 Rider J. E. Pike		
2	CIMBRIAN Mr. A. T. Creswick's b h ..	6 9 4	
	Devizes—Chersonese [L. Robertson]		
	Black, blue sash.		
	3 Rider D. Phillips		
3	VEILMOND Mr. E. Moss' br h	4 9 0	
	Limond—Veil [G. Price]		
	Green and black halves, black cap.		
	4 Rider Huse		
	LOUGHACON Mr. R. Miller's br m ..	6 8 13	
	Magpie—Charleville [W. Kelso]		
	Pale blue, black diamond, black sleeves yellow cap.		
	6 Rider		
5	CARRY ON Mr. J. S. Brunton's b m ..	4 8 9	
	Magpie—Farfadet [G. Price]		
	White, red sleeves and cap.		
	2 Rider McCarten		
6	JOHNNIE JASON Mr. W. J. Jones' b g 3	7 11	
	Treclare—Sweet Rosaleen [C. Unwin]		
	Purple and yellow stripes, yellow cap.		
	1 Rider J. Pratt		

Derby Day 1929 and W.S. Cox Plate Race Programmes.

A fine showing of Melbourne Cup Race programmes, and the 1931 programme.

A rare ticket to Phar Lap's last race, and a battered flyer for the 1932 film.

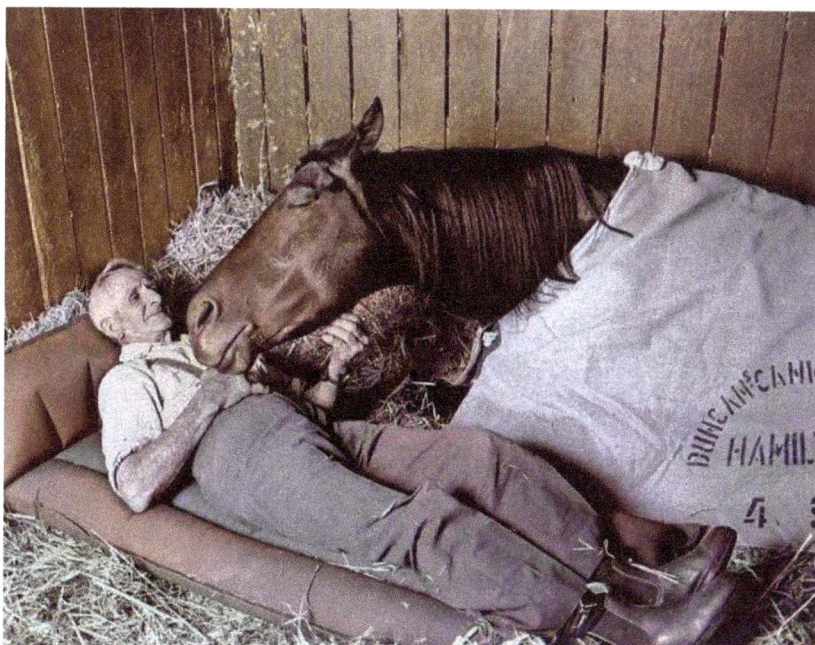

Phar Lap's Registration, December 1928.
Our final photo shows the late Tommy Woodcock, the eternal Strapper.

www.ingramcontent.com/pod-product-compliance
Lightning Source LLC
Chambersburg PA
CBHW041110110426
42740CB00054B/3445